A special thanks to Sarah E. Altman for her contributions to this story. It was her fabulous idea and her passion for empowering students with knowledge that made this book possible.

Copyright © 2024 Grow Grit Press LLC. All rights reserved. No part of this book may be reproduced in any form without permission in writing from the publisher. Please send bulk order requests to info@ninjalifehacks.tv

Paperback ISBN: 979-8-89614-010-8
Hardcover ISBN: 979-8-89614-012-2
eBook ISBN: 979-8-89614-011-5

Printed and bound in the USA.
NinjaLifeHacks.tv

Ninja Life Hacks®
by Mary Nhin

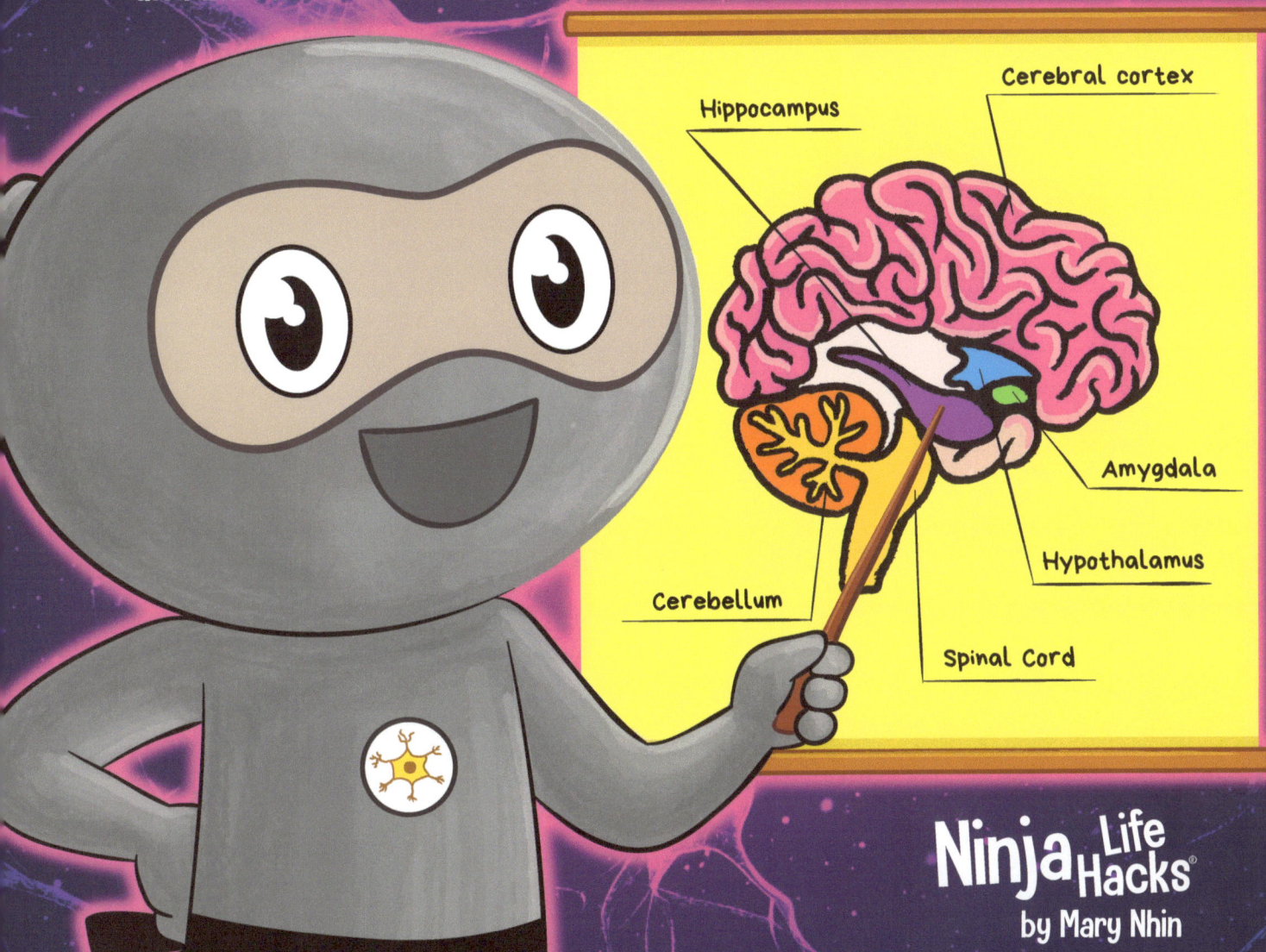

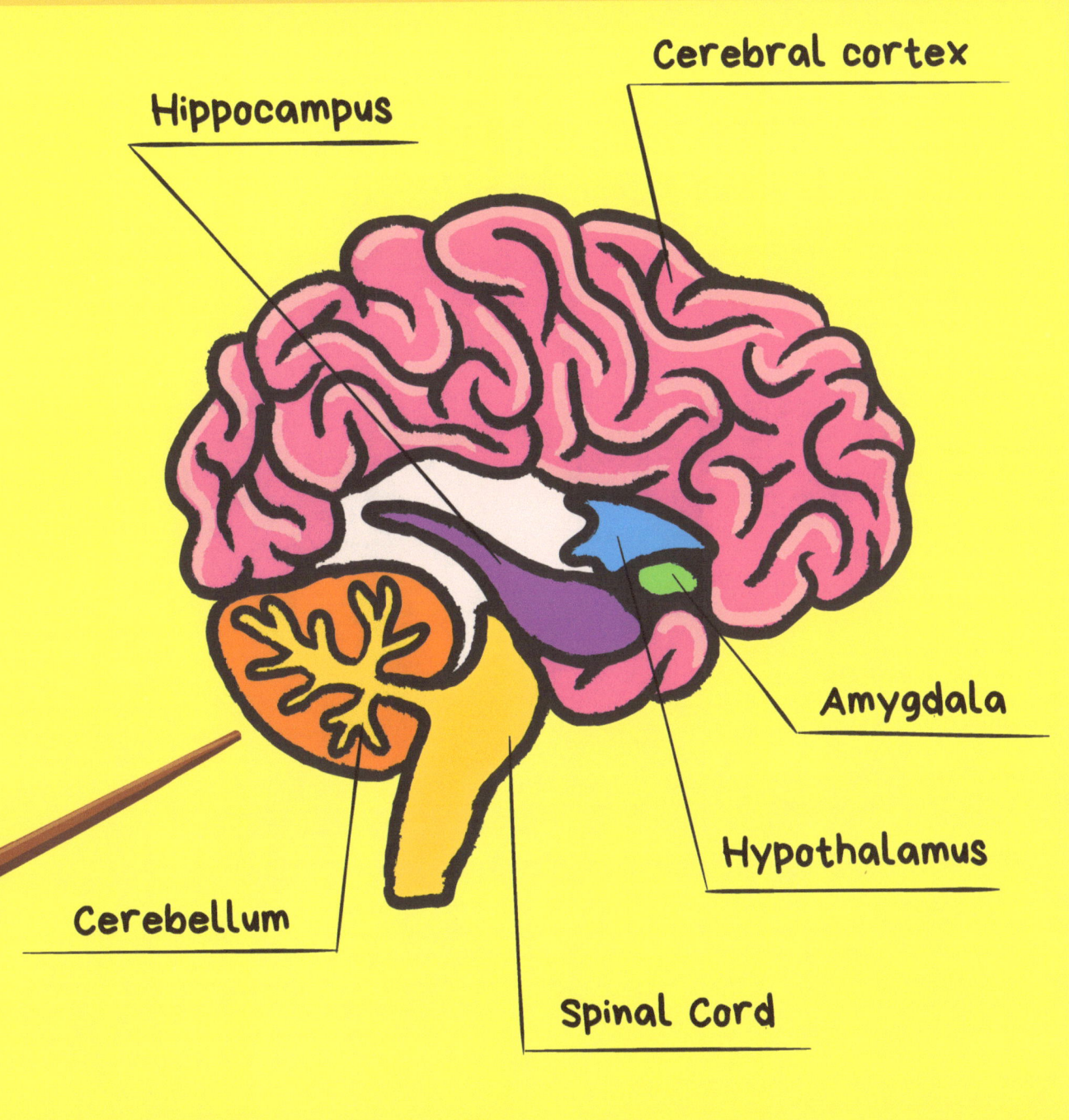

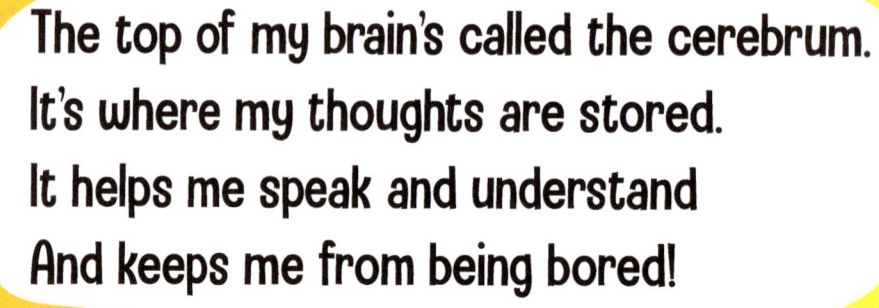

The brainstem works behind the scenes.
It helps me breathe and blink.
It keeps my heart and body strong
And even helps me wink!

The spinal cord is a long, strong rope.
It carries signals fast.
From brain to body, back and forth,
It makes my movements last.

Neurons are my brain's best friends.
They talk with speed and care.
They send signals far and wide
To my legs, toes, and hair.

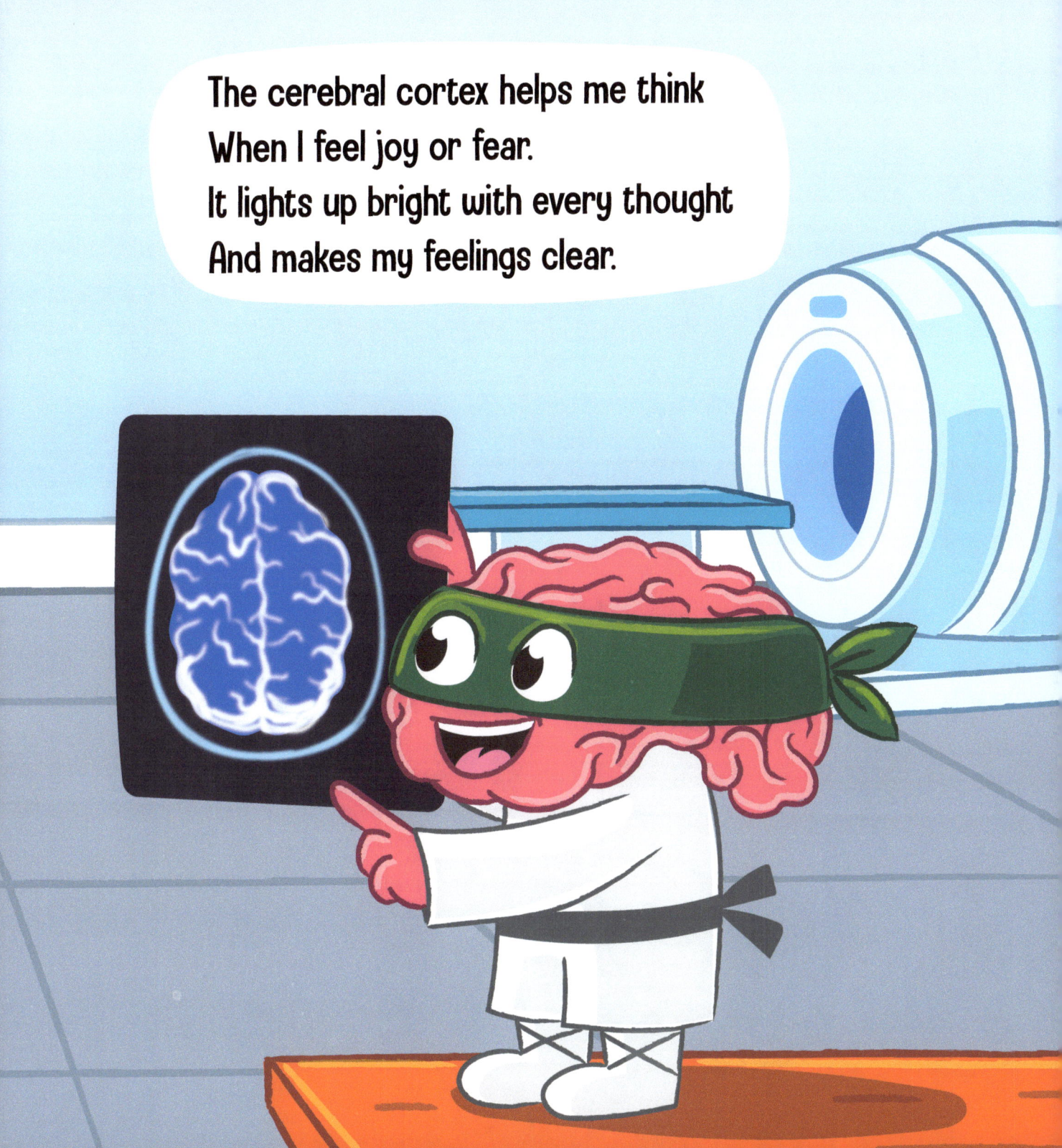

So take good care of your amazing brain.
It helps you every day.
I'm Neurologist Ninja—now you're set!
Let's think, explore, and play!

Check out the fun Neurologist Ninja lesson plans at ninjalifehacks.tv

I love to hear from my readers. Email me your feedback or thoughts on what my next story should be at info@ninjalifehacks.tv   Yours truly, Mary

 @marynhin   @GrowGrit
#NinjaLifeHacks

 Ninja Life Hacks

Mary Nhin   Ninja Life Hacks

 @officialninjalifehacks

www.ingramcontent.com/pod-product-compliance
Lightning Source LLC
LaVergne TN
LVHW070434070526
838199LV00015B/510